Tennis

Bernie Blackall

Heinemann Library
Des Plaines, Illinois

© 1999 Reed Educational & Professional Publishing
Published by Heinemann Library,
an imprint of Reed Educational & Professional Publishing,
1350 East Touhy Avenue, Suite 240 West
Des Plaines, IL 60018

03 02 01 00 99
10 9 8 7 6 5 4 3 2 1

Series cover and text design by Karen Young
Edited by Angelique Campbell-Muir
Photography by Malcolm Cross
Illustrations by Vasja Koman
Production by Alexandra Tannock
Printed in Hong Kong by Wing King Tong

Library of Congress Cataloging-in-Publication Data

Blackall, Bernie, 1956-
    Tennis / Bernie Blackall.
      p.   cm. -- (Top sport)
    Includes bibliographical references and index.
    Summary: Introduces the history, skills, rules, equipment, events,
and highlights of tennis.
    ISBN 1-57572-842-7 (library binding)
    1. Tennis--Juvenile literature. 2. Tennis--Australia--Juvenile
literature. [1. Tennis.] I. Title. II. Series: Blackall,
Bernie, 1956- Top sport.
GV996.5.B35 1999
796.342--dc21
                                      98-45918
                                           CIP
                                           AC

Acknowledgments

The publisher is grateful to the following for permission to reproduce
copyright material: Sport.The Library/Al Messerschmidt, p. 6 (Flushing
Meadows); David Callow, p. 6 (Melbourne Park); Sport-The Library/Maja
Moritz, p. 7 (Roland Garros); All Sport/Russell Cheyne, p. 7 (Wimbledon);
Coo-ee Historical Picture Library, p. 10 (Wimbledon in the 1920s);
Liles Photography, pp. 12, 18; All Sport/Gary Prior, pp. 8, 9.

Every effort has been made to contact copyright holders of any material
reproduced in this book. Any omissions will be rectified in subsequent
printings if notice is given to the publisher.

Some words are shown in bold, **like this.** You can find out what they mean by
looking in the glossary.

Contents

About Tennis

Tennis is played indoors or outdoors with a racket and a ball. The game is played on a court with a net across the center. The courts are usually marked with boundary lines painted on the court.

When two people play one another, it is a **singles** game. In singles, the inner set of **sidelines** marks the court boundaries.

A doubles match is a game with four people. Two pairs play against each other. In a doubles match, the outer sidelines are the boundary. The space between the doubles and singles sidelines is called the **doubles alley.**

A chair umpire oversees the game from a chair that places him or her close to the net and above the court. The chair umpire decides if a ball is in or out. Only an off-court judge can overrule the chair umpire.

The chair umpire is the top official on the court. He or she announces the score and oversees the linespersons. Linespersons are positioned along the lines around the court. Linespersons determine if a shot is in or out and if a **serve** is legal.

Ball girls and ball boys fetch and return the ball at the end of each play.

The tennis net hangs from a cable or chord between two posts located outside the doubles lines. They hold the net across the court. A narrow strap in the center holds the net tight. The net must be 3 feet (0.91 m) high at the center.

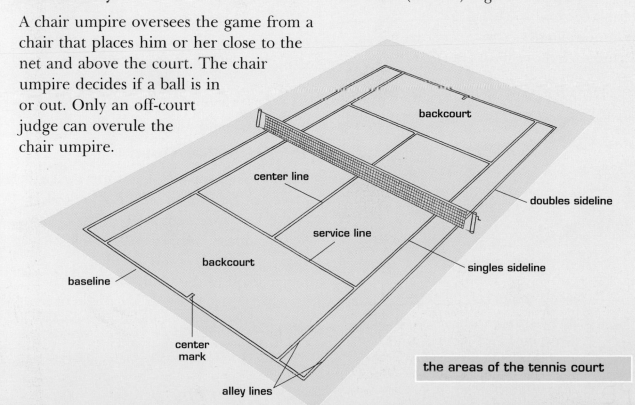

backcourt

center line

service line

backcourt

baseline

center mark

alley lines

doubles sideline

singles sideline

the areas of the tennis court

About Tennis

The Grand Slam

Four major international championships make up the **Grand Slam**:
- The Australian Open
- The French Open
- The Wimbledon Championships
- The US Open.

At each of these tournaments, competitions are held in different categories:
- men's singles
- men's doubles
- women's singles
- women's doubles
- mixed doubles
- junior singles (boys and girls)
- junior doubles (boys and girls)

The French Open is the only Grand Slam tournament played on clay courts.

A player who competes in and wins the same event at all four championships is said to have "completed the Grand Slam." In 1953, Maureen Connolly was the first woman to win the grand slam.

The Australian Open

Until 1987, the Australian Open was played in December on the grass courts of the Kooyong Tennis Club. Now, it is played in late January at the Melbourne Park stadium. It is the opening tournament of the Grand Slam. The Melbourne Park courts are made of a cushioned rubber and concrete mix called Rebound Ace.

The Australian Open is played at Melbourne Park. Center court has a roof that can be opened or closed depending on the weather.

The French Open

The French Championships date back to 1891. They have been played at Roland Garros since 1921. The French Open is played from late May through early June. The stadium is owned by the city of Paris. It is open to the public when the tournament is not being played.

The court surface is clay, so the ball bounces higher than it does on a grass court. Long **rallies**—sometimes up to 30 shots—are often played before a point is scored. **Baseline** players, those who play mostly ground strokes from the back of the court rather than close to the net, tend to dominate this tournament.

The Wimbledon Championships

The All England Lawn Tennis and Croquet Club in South London has hosted this tournament since 1877. It is played from late June to early July. As the oldest and most famous of the open tournaments, winning at Wimbledon is the high point of most players' careers.

The US Open at Flushing Meadows.

More than 15,000 fans jam into the stadium to watch the finals.

The courts at Wimbledon are grass. Since the ball can't bounce very high on grass courts, players have to quickly get in position to return the ball. Games on grass are played at a fast pace.

The U.S. Open

Held in early September, the U.S. Open has been played at Flushing Meadows, New York, since 1978. The stadium is located so close to New York's busiest airport that planes can be heard in the stadium.

The court surface is made of a type of rubberized concrete called Decoturf.

The worldwide media coverage and crowd attendance of the U.S. Open are second only to Wimbledon.

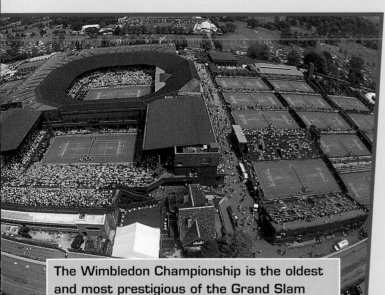

The Wimbledon Championship is the oldest and most prestigious of the Grand Slam events.

U.S. Highlights

Venus Williams

American players have contributed much to the popularity of the game of tennis today. They have been innovators, inspirations, and determined competitors.

Past heroes like Jack Kramer, Billie Jean King, Maureen "Big Mo" Connolly, Arthur Ashe, and others, paved the way for a new generation of U.S. tennis superstars.

The United States National Lawn Tennis Association was founded in 1881. The first U.S. men's tournament was held that year. Today the organization is known as the United States Tennis Association.

Tennis is popular throughout the world. The media gives the games and players a lot of coverage. All the major tournaments are broadcast live on television.

Davis Cup

In 1900, Dwight Filley Davis, of the United States donated the Davis Cup. The cup was to be awarded as a trophy each year to the country that won the world's men's championship. The first international competition was between the United States and Great Britain. By the First World War, France, Belgium, Austria, Australasia (Australia and New Zealand formed one team until 1923), Germany, and Canada had also entered the competition. More than 100 teams now take part in the annual Davis Cup competition.

Today, the Davis Cup is a men's competition played over three consecutive days. Two **singles** matches are held on the first day. A **doubles** match is played the second day. On the last day, two reverse singles matches are played. Reverse singles gives the players who didn't play against each other on the first day an opportunity to compete.

When the Davis Cup tournament began, there were not many others to play in. By 1981, however, there were so many competitions that the Davis Cup had to make some changes. Instead of taking weeks to play, it now takes days. In addition, the Davis Cup increased the amount of prize money.

Pete Sampras

Pete Sampras finished number 1 in ATP tour rankings in five straight years, becoming only the second player in history to accomplish this feat.

The greatness of Jimmy Connors, John McEnroe, Chris Evert, and Traci Austin stood to the challenge and introduced an entirely new personality to the game.

Goodbye polite-to-a-fault tennis. Hello grunts, temper tantrums, and raw competition.

The training and touring schedule of professional tennis players is beyond exhausting. Ask Andre Agassi or Lindsay Davenport, or any of the other winners of the 1996 Olympic gold medals in Atlanta, Georgia.

Powerful American players like Pete Sampras, Michael Chang, MaliVai Washington, Monica Seles, Venus Williams, and Lisa Redman work hard to keep their top spots in the game.

History g

Tennis is the best known and most
popular of all racket and ball games.
In the 1100 or 1200's, the French
invented a game called *Jeu de Paume,*
"game of the palm." Players hit the b
over a net with their palms. During
middle ages, *Jeu de Paume* spread to
It gained popularity in Britain in the
thirteenth century.

Real tennis

When rackets were introduced to th
game, players could hit the ball har
and faster. Before returning the ball
French players called out *"tenez"* as
courtesy to their opponents. As a re
the indoor game came to be called

Index